DIS

SPII

BY ANTHONY STRANO

ETERNITY INK

DISCOVERING SPIRITUALITY
Copyright © 1999
Brahma Kumaris Raja Yoga Centres (Australia)
Published by ETERNITY INK
78 Alt Street, Ashfield NSW 2131 Australia

Email: indra@one.net.au
First Edition August 1999

Strano, Anthony.
    Discovering spirituality.
    ISBN 0 9587230 6 0
    1. Yoga, Raja. 2. Spirituality. I. Title

    294.543

This book has been produced by The Brahma Kumaris World
Spiritual University, a non-profit organisation, with the aim of
sharing spiritual knowledge as a community service for the personal
growth of individuals. The Brahma Kumaris World Spiritual
University exists to serve the family of humanity: to assist individuals
to discover and experience their own spirituality and personal growth;
to understand the significance and consequences of individual actions
and global interactions; and to reconnect and strengthen the eternal
relationship with the Supreme Soul, the spiritual parent.

Contents

Giving

With habits, never give in or we lose our dignity.
With the self, never give up
      or we lose our destiny.
With others never give your worst
      or you will never develop your best.
The saying, "what we give is what we receive".
The lesson: Just to give.

Spirituality in everyday life

Spirituality is, in essence, knowing how to live. Through this knowing there is happiness. True spirituality is not a system of worship or ritual, but a positive attitude towards ourselves and others, which makes life a joy rather than a struggle.

The needs for a happy life can be simply fulfilling relationships and a sense of purpose. Happiness or a lack of it is not caused by external things, but comes from what is inside. For example, material well-being does not bring happiness, nor does it bring unhappiness.

The great disease of human consciousness is looking only to the external as a means of achieving happiness without examining personal values and attitudes, simply hoping for the best.

Happiness cannot be found by simply hoping for the best. There are no short cuts. No other person, no external thing can create a permanent state of well-being. Creating this is our own responsibility. Things from outside can contribute, guide and inspire, but ultimately life is what we make of it.

Exploring our deeper selves brings understanding. With this understanding we can begin to create the lives we wish to live. Without this understanding we cannot find release from crises.

Nowadays there seems to be a crisis, a dead-end or a disappointment at every turn. This seems almost to have become the standard for a human life.

When we are truly human, life is more than just surviving and overcoming obstacles. It is a joyful experience of love and meaning.

The quality of thought creates the quality of life

Think of a seed. It is like a point: small, tiny and compact, yet it holds all potential. A thought is like this. A thought is a seed. A seed that can be either positive or negative, depending on our mood, attitude and character. Thought creates feelings and attitudes. The combination of these is called consciousness. Human consciousness is the capacity to think, to reason, to feel and to express. All of this begins with just one thought.

Do we ever stop to observe our thoughts? Do we ever think of putting on the brakes, putting a full stop to our thoughts? Most of us allow them to scatter everywhere, wandering into every corner of our mind. Uncontrolled, scattered thoughts are like a speeding car: unless you brake, you'll crash. An uncontrolled mind is tense, worried and stressed. This causes a lot of damage.

We need to put on the brakes if our minds are

to work naturally. A natural mind is peaceful and a peaceful mind brings clarity. When we see things clearly there is no waste because we become mentally economical. The mind is not burdened with unnecessary thoughts. The biggest disease of the mind is over-thinking, especially too much thinking about others: what they did, what they should do, what they should have done, what they said, what you wished they'd said, why they spoke at all. All of these rob the mind of its inherent serenity.

Thinking too much is like eating too much. The heaviness makes it impossible to remain light and flexible. We get stuck on little things, and gradually the little things become huge things which we cannot shake off. Often when we think too much, we fantasise and overreact. Thus we create negative feelings.

It is far better to observe than to absorb every word, feeling and attitude, to get over-involved, or react too much. Observing gives us the patience and the clarity to think and act appropriately. Observing creates an inner focus that allows us to see reality.

We are constantly being influenced by the words and opinions of others. To bring peace back into our minds we need to journey inward. This re-balances us and stops us from wasting energy. We learn to think before speaking and to observe before acting. Without doing this the extremes of thought, speech and action eventually create disorder – emotionally, mentally and physically. This disorder brings tiredness, stress, restlessness and fear.

If we do not control ourselves, other people will. We do not like this. We react. We complain. Our tempers may explode. Unless we learn to journey inside and master ourselves, then others will definitely master us.

A brake on the mind means a brake on the tongue. Our thoughts and our words are closely connected, for what we think will lead to what we say. Our words – positive or negative – do affect others. If our words are harsh or critical, people react, giving back in turn what they received. This ping pong game of words and emotions occurs daily and is exhausting. Some days it is more like kick-boxing than ping pong!

As are our thoughts, so is our consciousness; and as our consciousness so is our life.

If we plant a positive, clean seed of thought and concentrate on it, we give it energy, like the sun gives to a seed in the earth. And as the seed in the earth awakens, stirs and begins to grow, the thoughts on which we concentrate awaken, stir and begin to grow. So let us sow positive thoughts.

Each morning before we begin the journey of our day let us sit still, in silence, and sow the seed of peace. Peace is harmony and balance. Peace is freedom – freedom from the burden of negativity and wastefulness. Let peace find its home within us. Peace is our original strength, our eternal tranquillity of being.

Let your first thought of the day simply be peaceful. Plant this seed. Water it with attention and you will gather the calm.

Learning

For spiritual development we need understanding. Deep understanding puts us in the right frame of mind. It leads to insight and gives us the capacity to perceive things in a totally new light. New perceptions clear out old, ineffective patterns, bringing a breath of new confidence to life.

Understanding, whether we call it knowledge, perception or insight, has great value, but only when we act upon it. It is action that brings experience. Experience, gained through practice, changes theory into reality. Reality creates inner strength. This is progress.

Clear understanding sometimes comes instantly, but more often it comes with time. Understanding is the foundation of learning.

In learning there is progress and in progress, joy. Let us keep learning and experimenting. For example, Leonardo da Vinci wanted to discover a way for people to fly. But his contemporaries insisted that, if God wanted human beings to fly,

He would have made them with wings, like the birds. That our place is on the ground. In spite of this, Leonardo kept on trying. Leonardo did try and though he failed, his determined attempts in the face of all opposition are still remembered today. Four hundred years later, the airport in Rome is named the Leonardo da Vinci airport.

We never know enough. There is always something to discover. There is always something new to learn.

Patience

Patience is the willingness to work with the process of growth. The good, the positive and the true cannot be attained immediately or automatically, they require time and some form of process. Sometimes we have to act, but sometimes we have to wait. People often try to force things to happen. Occasionally force works, but then we are not left with the feeling of true accomplishment. If every inch of success is gained through a battle or a conflict, the victory is hollow.

The best results do not only depend on ourselves or our own input. Success comes from learning to let things be: not just situations, but especially letting people be. I must certainly do , but I must not be attached to the doing itself. It is attachment to what we do that limits the success of the results, because the attachment or desire for particular results robs action of its purity.

How does the gardener work? The gardener selects his ground and, according to the season, plants the appropriate seeds. He likes his work: he tills the soil, sows the seed, then waters the plant; but, ultimately, he knows that it is up to nature to manifest her miracle of life. The gardener must always be attentive, making sure there is enough water, that the insects do not attack, but he cannot dominate the process. He cooperates and assists nature, but he must not interfere. The most beautiful garden is a product of the partnership between himself and nature; he aligns himself to her laws, understanding when to step in and when to wait.

True success is always based on a partnership. A real partnership recognises not only the role of the self but also the role of other people. We allow others to make their contributions without ignoring our own responsibilities. People forget to keep the balance.

The gardener has to understand the law of balance, otherwise he will do too much or too little, and the beauty and productivity of the garden will be diminished. The gardener has to have respect for time. He must have the patience to wait for the right season to plant his flowers, because if particular seeds are planted at the wrong time or in the wrong place, then no amount of attention will matter. Still, patience alone is not enough. Patience without understanding what is appropriate means that the waiting is not aligned to the truth of a situation.

Inactivity and patience are not the same thing. Inactivity could be apathy, and apathy comes when there is no desire to make effort or to commit yourself.

We should plant the seeds of right action and water them with responsibility and attention, but never force things because of self-centred desires. Selfish desires ruin the crop we wish to reap. There cannot be success in terms of happiness and well-being, if one is constantly interfering and manipulating what should be left alone. We must work with respect for the natural process. With this respect, the inherent good emerges from all things.

The power of faith

To be spiritual means to accept responsibility for personal change. A spiritual change can bring new horizons to our lives. There cannot be progress without change. Successful change brings the energy of inspiration and the enthusiasm to experiment and to persevere.

We should never give up hope, or think that the habits of the past are too entrenched. Positive thought, together with gentle perseverance, is capable of miracles. The impossible becomes possible.

Positive thought is based on real faith – a combination of spiritual understanding and experience. It is said that faith can move mountains. Faith is not blind hope or a convenient tradition camouflaging a lack of independent thinking. Nor is faith a justification for lack of understanding. Once we experience the dignity of our true selves then we develop faith in who we are in our right to the eternal inheritance of equality, freedom, happiness, and in our right to love and justice.

These rights can only be claimed through humility and with respect for the eternal laws of the universe. These rights manifest when we begin to identify with the truth of our spirituality. This new consciousness builds our faith in what we can be and what we can aim for.

Faith in spirituality enables us to trust ourselves. With trust we can let go of the past and have the courage to dare. To dare with courage gives us the confidence to know that we can achieve what we set out to achieve. If we begin with doubt then we have sown the seed of possible failure. Faith in spirituality always allows us to win. Every step of faith opens another chapter in our lives.

Honesty

Sometimes we try too hard to change for the better, sometimes we do not try hard enough. We do have to make an effort. Trying is necessary, if we want to improve. Our circumstances, our relationships and our destinies are only the echo of our own characters, so we are ultimately responsible. The only indispensable change we can make is in our own characters.

Commitment to improvement is necessary. The power of commitment is that it channels the energies available to us for the purpose of realising our goals. If we are honest with ourselves, we are committed to our growth.

We don't have to be perfect, but we do have to be honest. Honesty makes us realistic about what we can do and what we cannot. We only need to do our best according to our understanding and our capacity. Still, we must keep our eyes open to the next step on the ladder, never pressuring ourselves into climbing, if we are not yet ready, but always acknowledging the existence of that higher step. Being ready when it is time to climb. That is honesty.

Making honest efforts means we keep ourselves available for any of the lessons that life brings. For no matter how much we have read or done, no matter how much we know or understand, there is always room to learn.

Honesty requires humility.

Humility is not subservience

Humility means to be open to learning. Humility means to be open to change. Humility is only possible when we have self-respect, and self-respect can only come with self-knowledge. Self-knowledge tells us that we are part of the whole, like a spoke in a wheel.

We are not everything, nor are we nothing. It is humility which creates this understanding and keeps us in balance. If we are not attached either to our good qualities or our weaknesses, we can deal with both. Our positive qualities, through loving cultivation, will increase and serve others, and our weaknesses, through attention and honesty, will decrease.

Humility is our greatest protection. It prevents us from falling into the abyss of arrogance and self-complacency. Humility keeps us alert to all possibilities – from being deceived and creating disasters to the possibility of creating the most surprising miracles.

Humility is the fruit of self-respect, so a humble person is never afraid of being vulnerable and never fears loss. Humility brings certainty without dogma. What we need is always within us. Nothing – no one – can ever take these inner resources away. Humility springs from inner security, making us ready to communicate, to cooperate and to experiment with new thoughts and ideas.

Humility is the proof of self-mastery, of having conquered the 'I' and 'my' which snare a person into games of power, into games of manipulation which destroy and nullify respect and friendship.

We must be trustees, not owners, and we must act as such in connection with others. Ownership automatically creates the fear of loss. People who feel that they 'own' something or someone are always suspicious, always on guard. To be a trustee gives us the understanding that we own nothing and no one. Paradoxically, relinquishing everything, we receive everything.

What we need will come to us. There is enough for everyone.

'Trustee consciousness' means we save a tremendous amount of mental and emotional energy, because no time is wasted in selfish calculations or clever manipulations. With trustee consciousness, we become masters. A master works with the eternal principles of the universe. A master is humble and self-sufficient and maintains balance and harmony. The greatest humility of all is to recognise and accept that there are laws beyond those of human beings and that we are not the standard of the universe. Eternal principles protect and govern the well-being of all life. We, as individuals, need to align ourselves to these principles, for through alignment to eternal truths we find freedom. We find our way.

Alignment to divine laws does not limit or negate us. On the contrary, eternal laws are the means that allow the full expression of the individual self. There is no trespassing, as respect is always given to the individuality of others. Harmony is maintained.

With humility we recognise the right of all things to exist; to exist in peace; to exist in freedom; and to exist in happiness. This innate right is immortal law.

Subservience in relationships or to material objects is the result of fear; the fear of being ourselves; the lack of the courage to face, to change, to move in another direction. Self-respect releases us from fear. Self-respect releases us from dependence. When we do not think deeply enough for ourselves, we become subservient to social opinions and the people with whom we interact.

Humility brings introspection. We begin to examine the blocks and emotions that limit us. To break through subservience we have to learn to think for ourselves with honesty. Without humility, ego lures us and we are hypnotised by self-seeking desires.

Humility opens the door to self-knowledge. As we grow in self-knowledge, we grow in self-esteem. This self-esteem naturally creates a sense of identity. With this inner stability there is no fear of what is different. There is no desire to possess and accumulate. This is freedom. As one grows in this inner freedom, there is no desire to control people or situations. We know that the right things will happen in the right way at the right time. Humility is the other face of self-respect. The greater the humility, the greater the self-respect. No one, nothing is a threat. We are free.

A return to the roots

Roots are the hidden foundation, the support. All foundations are hidden and incognito and, though unseen, are responsible for holding up every structure. A building, no matter how new or old and no matter how beautifully built, requires a solid foundation if it is to remain standing.

A human being also has an invisible foundation. The body, the words and the actions, the visible structure of human life, have at their roots subtle energy. The process called 'death' occurs when this subtle energy leaves the human being. There is a mouth, but there are no words; there are eyes, but they do not see. There is a body, but there is no movement. The structure remains but the foundation has gone. The foundation of human life is not material.

Until we examine the roots of our human existence, we cannot begin to understand and change ourselves. Psychology has attempted to reach these roots and has helped us understand the inner world of both our subconscious and conscious patterns. However, to truly know ourselves we must return to the seed.

For human beings, thoughts are the seed. Thoughts spring from the soul – a point of non-material energy, eternal in form and identity. The soul is not subject to change as is the body. The soul, which is not of the material world, is the foundation of consciousness; this living, non-physical vessel holds our personality, our thoughts, our desires and our emotions.

Just as the seed of a tree holds its image deep within until appropriate conditions permit its manifestation, the soul holds within the image of individual personality manifesting through action.

On a spiritual path we attempt to reach what is eternal in human personality. Irrespective of the negativity we have accumulated within , our basic nature is pure.

The soul – that is the true self – is not originally sinful, it is originally good. To be on the spiritual path means we will experience this original goodness. When this precious energy is experienced, there is a leap of consciousness. In history this leap has been known as illumination. Illumination is the leap to new insight that gives confidence and hope. Then there is more reality in life and, consequently, more happiness. We are renewed.

Raja yoga meditation

Habits, the deep addictions of the soul, like emperors who own a kingdom, rule us. Habits, over time, gain supremacy over logic and reason, doing as they like without thinking or caring for the true well-being of the person. The mind is the throne of these emperors and, like tyrants, they usurp peace and clarity. They domineer without sweetness or sympathy.

The aim in Raja Yoga meditation is to change our habits and to dethrone these tyrants. To do this, we need an intellect filled with spiritual knowledge. We need to use this third eye of understanding. Through knowledge, reason returns to the human soul and gives it the power to conquer the tyrants of the mind.

Knowledge is necessary, but silence is also necessary. In silence we can make connection with God, which gives us the strength to regain our lost dignity. Our original dignity lies in being the ruler of ourselves. Raja Yoga is about learning to master ourselves, regaining our inner kingdom and regaining our throne.

The wonder of silence

In silence lies the ability to listen: to listen to ourselves, to others and to God.

Listening is a lost art. Without it we cannot communicate, we cannot relate to each other and so we cannot live life meaningfully. We need to learn to listen.

Sitting in silence allows us to listen to ourselves and to understand. This silence can heal. The worries, the pain can be healed when we listen. Spiritual medicine is ever-present in the soul. Whenever we need it, to whatever extent we need it, we can find it within.

The disease of anger needs the medicine of tolerance; the pain of disappointment needs the medicine of hope; the violence of revenge and spite needs forgiveness; fear needs courage; ego needs self-respect. Through inner silence we receive the strength to heal.

Truly listening means that we can perceive reality. We see our real selves in silence. If we are still and silent, if we step within, we see the blueprint of our original goodness, our true selves.

Ego, anger, fear and wrong desires have created the variety of sicknesses within our minds and within our hearts. These sicknesses are not part of our true selves and we have believed in them for too long. The mixing of our original goodness with this acquired negativity has caused a lot of confusion. To separate and to dissolve this sickness of negativity we need the qualities of our original selves – especially the qualities of love and peace.

These original qualities cleanse and heal. Every day we become cleaner, every day we become truer to ourselves. It is in the mirror of silence that we see our original self. It is in the mirror of silence that our spiritual identity becomes a reality rather than a distant hope. To consolidate this reality, we must create a daily space for silence. We must listen to ourselves.

Once we've learnt to listen to ourselves, then we will enjoy listening to others. Listening creates closeness, and closeness allows for friendship. What is life without friendship? What we offer from the heart creates the quality of our relationships. A genuine relationship is based on sincerity. A genuine relationship is enduring and constant. This makes life worthwhile. This is the love that sustains. This is the love that nutures.

Listening to God is the most sublime experience possible for a human being. In silence we can feel God loving us – a love that heals and a love that frees. God is the One whose friendship gives us back to ourselves. This is the relationship that makes us authentic. His love is selfless and never possessive. His love never diminishes us. God's love is pure.

Pure love heals the most shocking of wounds. This unique love is only found in the stillness of silence. We can only experience this love when we are not demanding or calculating a response. Selfishness blocks the heart.

Knowing God

God is Pure Truth. God expresses Himself in the purest and the most benevolent way. This is called divine Love. He is this for eternity. God is not the prerogative of a particular people or religion. God belongs to us all. God's vision has no borders.

God is light. God is a point of light, an immortal essence radiating light. As the source of reality, God is the standard for true life. True life is life as it should be lived by human beings – with freedom, with happiness and with love.

The physical sun sends rays of golden light and warmth to the seeds in the earth. When the seeds absorb the light and the warmth they begin to stir, to awaken, and the miracle of life occurs. In the same way, God, the source of Light, emanates rays of love constantly. If we are spiritually alert, we receive those rays. Then our original goodness awakens within us.

This is the season of awakening. In spring the sun gives extra light and warmth to the earth, enabling the flowering of nature. At this time, God, the Sun of Knowledge, is radiating pure energy to us. This divine energy reconciles both human souls and nature, returning them to their original state of harmony. A springtime in human civilisation is about to bloom. A civilisation of true and pure human beings, like gods on earth. We will see again the lost Eden, the sunken Atlantis, the forgotten Paradise.

To receive this divine love all we need to do is remember the Eternal One, the Source – God. This releases us from the past. This allows a renaissance of the spirit, the birth of the new humanity.

Purity and happiness

To be pure allows us to rejoice in what we are. Purity is not a denial of life but an affirmation of life's original dignity and worth. Recognising that people, our brothers and sisters, are also heirs to life and intrinsically good brings a flow of joy to the heart.

Purity is the eye of Truth through which we see all things as they were originally meant to be – clean, clear, free and unique. Purity brings such positivity of vision that, whilst we are aware of the realities of negativity, we are able either to neutralise them or to go beyond them. Purity brings compassion, transforming where it can. Then we no longer criticise or complain. When we are pure, we are happy. Happiness is being content with who we truly are.

Purity of vision means having no bad feelings or negative reactions when we are criticised. People with pure feelings can flow in and out of situations without being damaged and without damaging; this gives them the capacity to be independent. If we have too much ego, then we get hurt easily and react by withdrawing or becoming aggressive.

Purity brings independence. The proof of that independence is the ability to love and to come close to others. When there is purity, others are not afraid of us nor are we afraid of anyone, because there is no threat of loss or damage, only pure love. Pure love recognises the inherent individuality of every person and respects it. There is no labelling and no neat categorising.

God never labels us. Whether we are male or female, Muslim, Jew or Christian, whether we are Chinese, Greek or Indian, God sees and respects each of us as unique human beings in this drama of life. Our purpose is to express this uniqueness as clearly and naturally as possible.

Since God knows our eternal uniqueness, He never tries to make us anything other than what we are. It is in being what we are, that our happiness lies. As the benevolent source of Love, God gently encourages the discovery of our uniqueness.

With God's love, we realise that we do not need to borrow strength or identity from anyone or anything else. Our anchor for life is internal. With this insight, nothing can diminish our sense of worth.

Truth

Truth is power. Truth is strength. Strength is an inner store of resources which keeps us mentally, emotionally and spiritually healthy.

Contentment is a great strength. It comes when a person lives in honesty and simplicity. Contentment means we have overcome useless desires. It is said that you can discern a person's truth from their level of contentment.

To develop our inner strength, we need honesty. Honesty means that truth is practised in daily life. Without honesty, illusions rule. The greater the illusions, the weaker we become.

Whatever knowledge we have, if we are not honest, we do not realise that we must look inside ourselves to find what needs to be changed. It is honesty that focuses our attention on ourselves, instead of others.

Where there is honesty, there no laziness, fear or dependence. Laziness is the attachment to what is comfortable, to convenient ways of thinking. There is no deep desire to change. The consciousness cannot rise to what is noble, because it is addicted to its own familiar routines.

Fear is only lack of understanding. Fear comes from being dependent. We are sometimes afraid simply because something is unfamiliar. When people are honest, they are willing to change, because their security does not come from conditioning or society's norms it comes from deep within themselves. People with truth know they cannot lose; they can only learn.

The more a person depends on a pattern of thinking, a particular person or a particular role, the more there is the fear of loss. The security created by dependence is illusion. The reality of life is that anything external to ourselves can, at any time, vanish. What will we do then? Where is our life's anchor? If it is not within, we will suffer.

Dependence does not create a good relationship. It creates bondage. To think that another human being can absolutely fulfill us is as absurd as ducks drinking tea! A relationship based on dependence has no truth in it, which is why there is fear and discontent. We overreact and we imagine and little things become exaggerated.

People with inner strength keep things in perspective. Keeping things in perspective enables us to handle them more effectively.

Laziness, fear and dependence use the same vocabulary. "I cannot", "I do not know where", "I do not understand", "if", "maybe", "sometimes", "never", "perhaps", "tomorrow", "next year". These are the words we use to excuse ourselves or to put things off. This attitude can never give us strength.

Usually, inner strength brings external power that is the ability to brings thoughts into action. This power is never rough or dominating, but gentle and firm without trampling over the feelings of others.

Blame

Some people blame themselves for everything. Whatever goes wrong they assume it is their fault. A lack of self-respect makes them believe themselves to be unworthy. Over time these feelings of unworthiness manifest themselves in the idea that they deserve neither happiness nor love and that their sorrow and suffering is a deserved punishment. They lose the strength and vision to seek solutions.

Some people constantly project the cause of their misfortunes on others. The main reason for projecting blame is an unwillingness to take responsibility for our own choices. It is more comfortable and more convenient to make someone else the scapegoat. People hold onto the past and cannot forgive or forget. They miss the opportunity to change their ways of thinking, they lose the opportunities of the present.

Problems and difficulties are signals that we need to change our attitudes and our behaviour. We need to acknowledge our weaknesses and take responsibility for the choices we make. When we take responsibility, we win freedom.

Other people are neither the cause of, nor the solution to our unhappiness. We will never find solutions if we are preoccupied with blaming others. Our minds will be too full of resentment, animosity and hopelessness to have the clarity to choose wisely.

In blaming others we justify our own lack of responsibility; in blaming ourselves we justify our feelings of guilt and inferiority.

Spirituality gives us the wisdom to transcend both.

The power of forgiveness

The ability to forgive others depends on how honest we are with ourselves. Have we journeyed through this life pure, perfect and clean with never a wrong thought, a wrong word or action? If we look at ourselves honestly, then how can we not forgive another? When we face our own shortcomings, then our anger against others disappears.

In the past we have all acted wrongly, either because of not knowing what is right, or out of fear or misunderstanding. Looking back on the past, most of us regret many things that we have said or done. With time and knowledge we realise what is right and begin to make amends. Just by having the desire to to do this we begin this process of our own forgiveness. If this process is to progress, we have to forgive others. We cannot condemn others and excuse ourselves. This is cheating and the universe will not allow it.

The power to forgive comes from compassion. Forgiveness dissolves the compulsive need to prove ourselves right. It removes the indignation we feel at imagined injustice.

If we do not learn to forgive, resentment will poison us. Those who do not forgive, who insist on playing the role of the judge, must expect the same in return, what else?

When we do not forgive, we carry a double burden: both the resentful thoughts of others' injustice and the hidden reality of our own injustice. Forgiveness releases us from these bitter emotions.

Forgiveness means to compassionately and peacefully move forward with what is good, towards what is better. Forgiveness melts the hardness of another's heart. Our forgiveness, at first, may be puzzling them. People may even think of us as naive, but eventually they will appreciate and esteem this supreme act of kindness.

To forgive and forget is love in action. But we must learn to forgive ourselves, as well as others, otherwise the process of releasing this burden neither begins nor progresses. Our freedom is totally blocked.

Forgiving ourselves means letting go of the past. But it also means not making the same mistakes again and again, not inventing convenient ways to excuse ourselves. Even God's forgiveness and compassion cannot be felt by the person who has hardened his own heart against others. If we want to be forgiven, then we must be willing to forgive first. The courage to act first is the true sign of the one who is truly just. The one who forgives first not only proves his justice, but especially proves his love.

The spirit of generosity

Generosity means more than just giving. It also means to cooperate with others. The greatest act of generosity is to see beyond the weaknesses and mistakes of others, helping them to recognise their innate value.

The truly generous are those who have made the effort to master themselves. Such people have a capacity for generosity, because they understand the deep personal work required to achieve the good. They empathise, because they understand the difficulties faced by those who attempt the goal of self-knowledge. The generous are also benevolent towards those who choose to ignore or even to criticise the good. It is understood that the necessity for the good cannot be ignored indefinitely.

Those who have never tried to improve themselves have little, if any, tolerance towards others. Never having faced their own shortcomings, they cannot respond to the shortcomings of others with understanding. Their hearts are stingy.

When we give or share with the wrong intention then whatever we do will never be satisfying. We may feel that others are ungrateful, insensitive, or even selfish, but the real problem is that we do not recognise our own selfish motives. If the central motive of our life is wanting to get something, then assuredly we will never get anything. At least, not anything of lasting value.

It is when we unselfishly offer our personal resources, including time and virtues, that we receive. Love and respect must be freely given, thus cannot be demanded. Authentic goodness is measured by the capacity to be genuinely good with everyone. To share the good is the expression of a generous nature.

The greatest treasures of life are love, peace and happiness. The only way to increase these treasures, is to give them away. Even if we have only a little bit of one of these treasures, if we give it, we will see it grow. For example, if we have not much patience but use the little we do have, our ability to be patient will grow.

Generosity of spirit increases everything we have and simultaneously gives us everything we need. If we are stingy, we lose; everything inside us decreases. When people are stingy they try to accumulate; they have a passion for collecting as much as they can, both emotionally and materially. Sometimes they will go to unhealthy extremes, but at the end of all the effort and struggle there is a great poverty of spirit. The mind and heart feel empty.

As human beings, we have deep emotional needs. We cannot satisfy these through accumulation but only through authentic generosity.

Love and knowledge

There are many habits and attitudes which are too ingrained, too tightly wound into the personality, to be removed solely on the basis of knowledge. Knowledge is necessary and the first step towards personal freedom, but it is not enough to effect practical change, no matter how clear and inspirational it is.

Without love one moves along trying to improve only on the basis of the knowledge of what is right and wrong. This gradually imprisons the self in a cage of strict effort, so instead of opening and releasing ourselves we close and trap ourselves.

It is love from God that enables us to accept ourselves as we are and to equally accept the necessity for personal change. We accept this because divine love always motivates us to aim for the highest in ourselves.

Love inspires us to reach the highest, and at the same time, removes the pressure of strict effort, by allowing for mistakes and weaknesses.

Through God's love we form a friendship with time. Time does not threaten us any more. Time does not hurry us, but works with and for us. We realise how precious time is, therefore we do not wish to waste it by neglecting the opportunities it is giving us to change.

God's love frees us quickly and effectively, because it allows us to see and work with the positive side of ourselves. When we see only the negative, we become afraid, so we suppress our weakness, not wanting to acknowledge it and not wanting others to see us as weak.

If we only have the theory of spiritual knowledge and work only with our intellects, then there will be lack of confidence, fear of failure and even arrogance. To change successfully, we need both spiritual knowledge and divine love.

For progress we need divine cooperation, accepting it with responsibility and not attempting to offload everything onto God. We have to do our part.

Love creates trust. Trust in ourselves gives us the opportunity to see, through God's eye, our original worth and value. All we have to do is to remember Him.

All we need is the constant awareness of our original divine state and the remembrance of the Eternal One, whose guiding love makes everything possible.

Balance

Becoming spiritual is not a matter of learning techniques, chanting words or performing rituals. Spiritual growth means learning to keep balance. With balance we gain perspective, we keep a hold of reality, and we learn to avoid extremes. Extremes segregate and separate. In balance there is reconciliation, even with those things that appear to be opposites.

People who are spiritually aware understand that the myriad threads that run through everything in this universe are each necessary. It is all these diverse threads woven together that create the wondrous tapestry of existence. Balance is what holds the diverse threads peacefully and harmoniously. The measure of a person's practical wisdom is their capacity for balance. Balance is harmony and order, it is peace.

In the modern world, keeping balance is not always easy: just one negative thought or word can throw us totally off balance. We are like tightrope walkers. To successfully walk to the other side, we carefully place one foot after the other, holding a pole to balance. A slightly wrong step, a little too heavy on one side of the pole, then over we topple. The rope we walk is the path to our destination. To reach the other side, each of our steps must be accurate. Each step requires that we balance the different virtues. There should not be too much of one virtue on one side otherwise we can lose our balance. For example, in life we need to be sweet. Sweetness is a sign of a good and understanding nature. However, too much sweetness, like honey, is sticky. People stick to us or we stick to them, then the heaviness overbalances us.

Even positive things need to be in balance. For example, we need to be determined to achieve our aims. Determination provides the energy and concentration necessary for any accomplishment. However, too much of the wrong kind of determination can become stubbornness and the narrow vision that makes people insensitive to others. So determination needs to be balanced with patience and flexibility.

Every virtue when in action has value and is necessary, but it requires some level of detachment if a balance is to be kept. If we carry a virtue to the extreme it can become a negative thing. With detachment everything remains in balance. Attachment, or wanting something too much, destroys a good thing. Attachment, even to the good qualities in one's self, reduces the value of that goodness. We become dominated by ego, the original purity is gradually lost.

There are many other qualities and virtues necessary in life that require balance. We need to be strong-hearted to face the many difficult situations of life, but we must never be so hard-hearted that we are not concerned for the sorrow of others. We should become content by appreciating what we have in life, but never become complacent so that we make no effort to improve. We should be flexible, with tolerance and humility, but never compromise our principles, thus losing our integrity. We should be concerned about others but never worry about them. Worry comes from fear, and worrying never brings solutions. To be concerned is to care, but to help we need to be clear minded and free from fear.

We should be spontaneous but never impulsive. If people are impulsive they act without thinking. Impulsive emotions can be very negative. Pure feelings of love and joy, if they are genuine, are natural and spontaneous. Spontaneity is positive and uplifting.

We must challenge but never provoke. For progress and positive change, we need to challenge ourselves and others to think and to act in new and different ways. Provocation, on the other hand, is based on ridicule. Ridiculing and deriding what others believe or do is destructive and never beneficial.

We must be lawful but not dogmatic. Laws are necessary. As members of humanity we need to do what is right and fair in order to protect the well-being of all things. However, even though we need laws, we must never lose sensitivity to the needs of the individual. To be obedient to eternal laws creates compassion. It never means becoming dogmatic and fundamentalist.

These balances that make life peaceful and happy. Balance is acquired when there is discernment. Discernment comes from wisdom and personal experience and the right discernment gives us the appropriate understanding at the appropriate time.

Freedom, justice and love

The law for every human being is : 'How we treat others is how we will be treated, equally and the same'. This is justice. Love naturally respects freedom and the choice or right of each person to be who they are. Love is the ultimate justice.

Freedom is the right to choose. Without choice the individual cannot enjoy life. We are happy when we are free to choose. Human history is filled with wars, revolutions and declarations for freedom, independence and liberation. For human beings, freedom is the most cherished right; it allows the full expression of every individual's hopes, aims and aspirations.

Freedom is an innate personal right; but when it is misused, the result is sorrow of one kind or another. Sorrow is the language of justice. We are totally free to choose. This is an eternal law and our right, but we should never forget that above personal free choice there is also the eternal law of justice. The main purpose of justice is not to punish but to uphold the rights and freedom of all human beings and nature. Justice is benevolent for it constantly strives to preserve the inherent balance and harmony of the universe.

It is the misuse of freedom which creates injustice. Consequently, the role of eternal justice is to heal that injustice, to correct that imbalance. Inevitably where there is injustice there is violence – violence that is physical, verbal or emotional. When any person is not permitted their innate right to be, the outcome is violence. To disrespect and destroy another's right to be, is the greatest violence of all.

The religion of today's world is violence. This is the result of selfish choices. The violence of people towards each other and against nature is so great that we can see and feel the machinery that clears these injustices working at colossal speed. This is evidenced by great upheavals in the mind and great chaos in the world. In this turmoil, continual unjust thoughts and actions are producing a hurricane of negativity.

Humanity has misused its freedom. But in the eye of the storm, serene justice works to redress all imbalance.

No human thought, opinion or action can overrule justice. Her law is absolute. The law is that harmony and order must be preserved both at a personal and universal level. When misuse of freedom produces disorder, then justice, with or without humanity's consent, strives to regain the balance. This regaining of balance can cause pain to individuals who refuse to change their selfish attitudes. Unless they open their minds and hearts to understanding, the pain continues.

Justice is absolutely infallible because her ultimate purpose is to preserve the good for all. Justice is not the same as punishment. Justice is the simultaneous process of realisation and responsibility. We have freedom and we have rights, but we need to realise that we are responsible for the consequences of the way we use those rights. Nature herself reacts with upheavals, attempting to maintain her innate harmony in spite of the constant, selfish interference of the human race. If there has been any imbalance, justice will, without request, reinstate balance.

Even God, the highest authority, does not judge or punish. Punishment is the automatic process of universal rebalancing working itself out through time. In fact we should not really call it punishment. It is simply eternal justice.

Even greater than justice, there is one power that can cancel the debts, redress the imbalances and heal the sorrow. This power respects justice because justice works perfectly, but it can overrule her law of 'an eye for an eye, a tooth for a tooth'. That power is love. In its perfect pure form that power is called Divine Love and it comes from God. With great compassion Divine Love cancels the past, dissolves all debts and releases the human soul. Divine Love never accuses and never shames us but wants to release us. The past is past.

However, love is active only on one condition. That condition is that we must forgive others to the extent that we wish to be forgiven. If that condition is broken, then automatically justice will assume her responsibility.

To love others selflessly is to acknowledge and respect their right to exist as they are. We accept them. If we return to the same old habit of using freedom irresponsibly, and interfering selfishly, then there is no recourse for justice other than to come into play.

About the author

Anthony Strano is the director of Brahma Kumaris in Athens, Greece. Born in Australia in 1951, he graduated from Macquarie University in Sydney with a Bachelor of Arts and a Diploma of Education.

A spiritual seeker all his life, Anthony became a student of the Brahma Kumaris in 1977. Now, years later, he is one of the Spiritual University's most dedicated and experienced teachers.

Over the years, he has travelled widely, sharing the knowledge he's gathered. He has run seminars and workshops throughout Europe and Australia on positive thinking and stress-free living, on education and values, on science and spirituality – in fact, on all areas of human development.

Organising three international symposia on Science and Consciousness in Athens from 1990 to 1993 and another in Mexico in 1994. Anthony has also run similar seminars on the island of

Paros. These were for professional people from many areas of expertise to explore positive thought and consciousness.

An arts festival, organised by Anthony and dedicated to the United Nations International Year of Poverty in 1996, demonstrated how the exploration of the ways in which theatre, literature, music and fine arts can be tools for overcoming poverty of the spirit.

His own spiritual journey at the heart of his existence, Anthony considers himself always to be a student as well as a teacher.

Other Eternity Ink meditation books, tapes and CDs available.
For a catalogue contact:
Eternity Ink, 78 Alt Street Ashfield NSW Australia 2131
Tel +61 2 9990 7333 Fax +61 2 9799 3490
Email: indra@one.net.au
www.bkwsuau.com *or* www.bkwsu.com

ETERNITY INK

Eternity Ink is publisher for the Brahma Kumaris World Spiritual
University. If you wish to find out about the free meditation
courses offered by the Brahma Kumaris World Spiritual
University, contact the main centre closest to you:

UK:	International Co-ordinating Office, 65 Pound Lane, London, NW10 2HH, UK, Tel (20) 8727 3350
AUSTRALIA:	78 Alt Street, Ashfield, Sydney NSW 2131 Tel (2) 9716 7066
BRAZIL:	R. Dona Germaine Burchard, 589 – Sao Paulo, SP 05014-010, Tel (11) 864 3694
HONG KONG:	17 Dragon Road, Causeway Bay, Tel (852) 2806 3008
INDIA:	25 New Rohtak Road, Karol Bagh, New Delhi, 1100055, Tel (11) 752 08516
KENYA:	PO Box 12349, Maua Close, off Parklands Road, Westlands, Nairobi, Tel (2) 743 572
RUSSIA:	35, Prospect Andropova, Moscow 15487 Tel (95) 112 51 28
USA:	Global Harmony House, 46 South Middle Neck Road, NY 11021, Tel (516) 773 0971